S0-BYI-571

MICHAEL JACKSON NUMBER ONES

Produced by
Alfred Music Publishing Co., Inc.
P.O. Box 10003
Van Nuys, CA 91410-0003
alfred.com

Printed in USA.

ISBN-10: 0-7390-6547-5
ISBN-13: 978-0-7390-6547-1

CONTENTS

BAD

Written and Composed by Michael Jackson
Arranged by Dan Coates

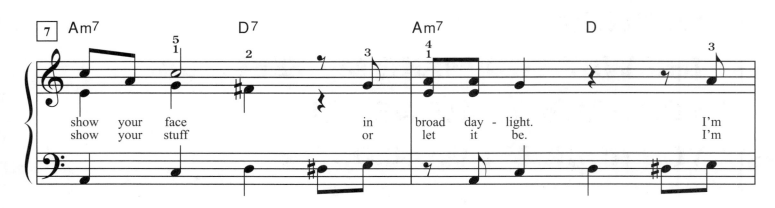

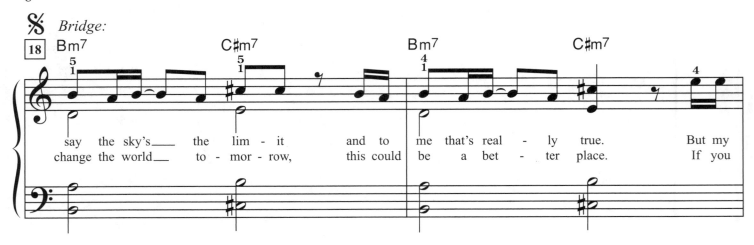

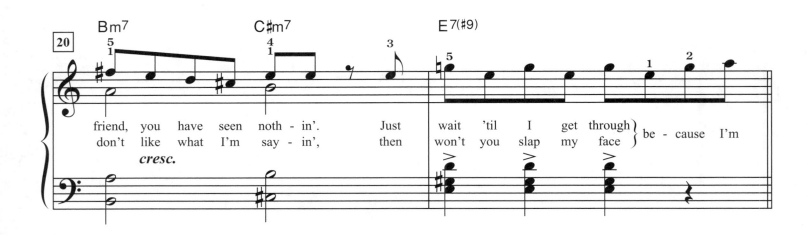

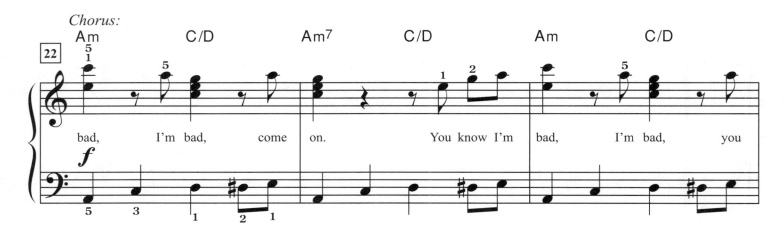

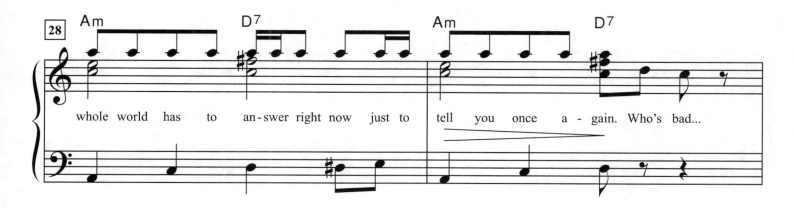

whole world has to an-swer right now just to tell you once a-gain. Who's bad...

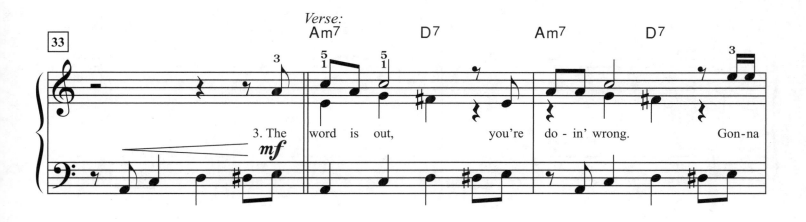

Verse:

3. The word is out, you're do-in' wrong. Gon-na

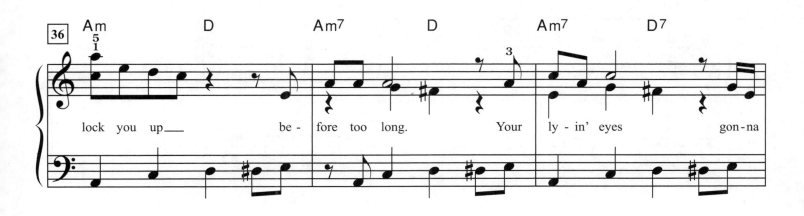

lock you up___ be-fore too long. Your ly-in' eyes gon-na

BEAT IT

Written and Composed by Michael Jackson
Arranged by Dan Coates

Moderately bright

Verse:

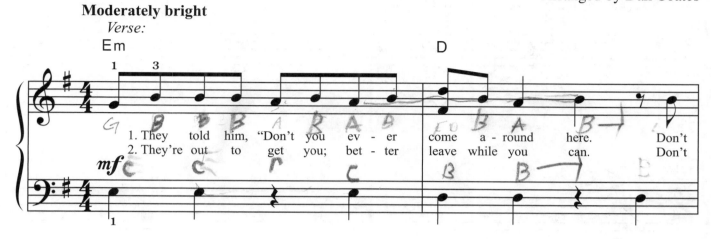

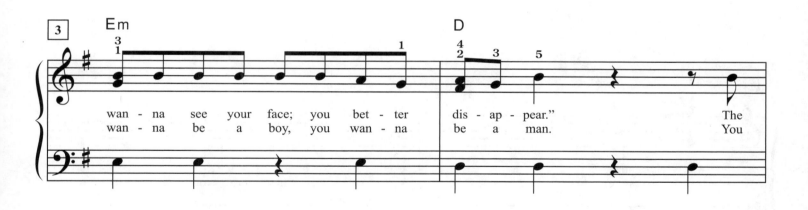

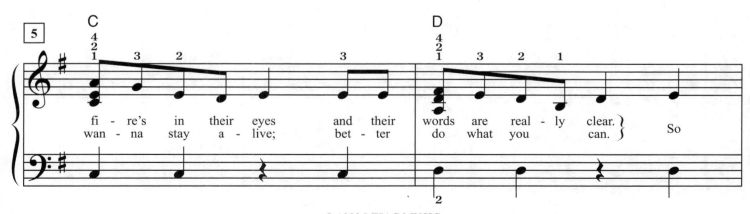

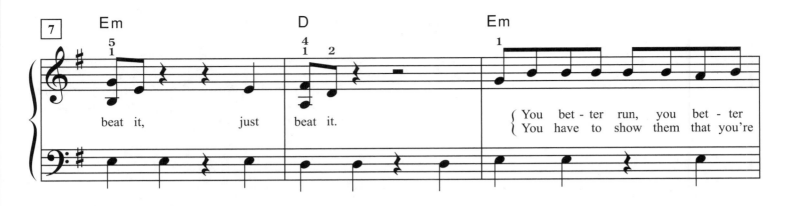

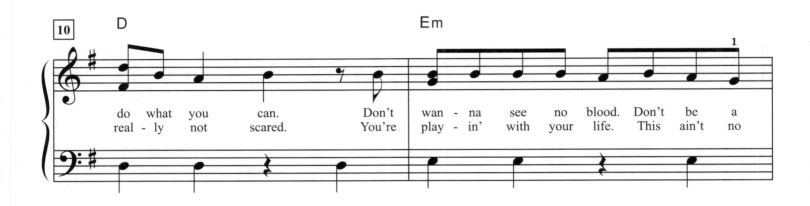

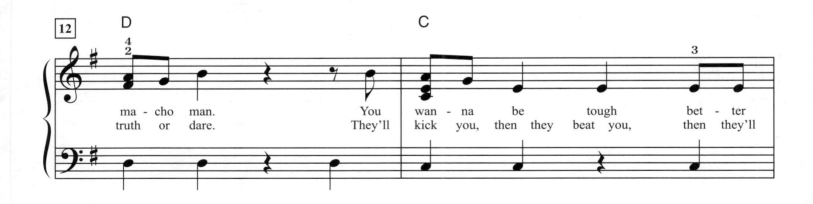

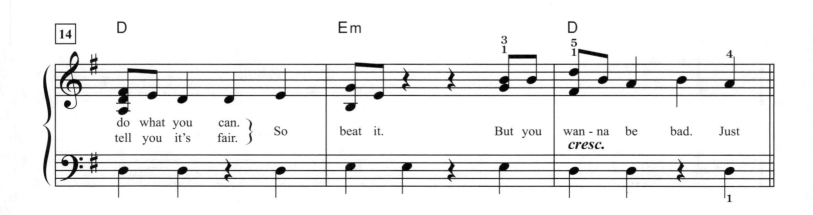

Chorus:

beat it,___ beat it.___ No___ one wants to be de - feat -

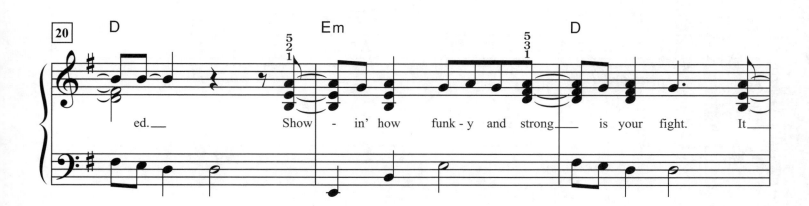

ed.___ Show - in' how funk - y and strong___ is your fight. It___

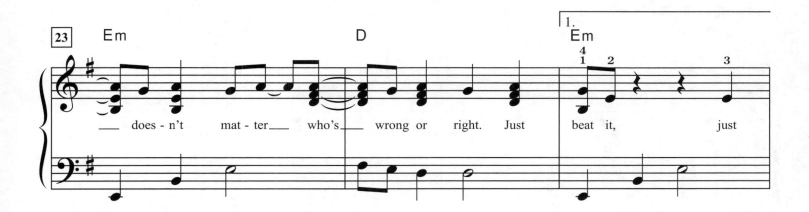

___ does - n't mat - ter___ who's___ wrong or right. Just beat it, just

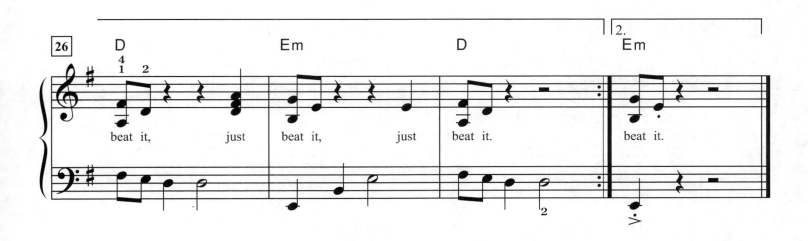

beat it, just beat it, just beat it. beat it.

BEN

Words by Don Black
Music by Walter Scharf
Arranged by Dan Coates

BILLIE JEAN

Written and Composed by Michael Jackson
Arranged by Dan Coates

Steady rock beat

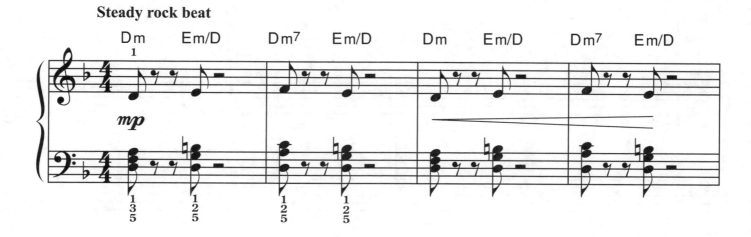

Verse:

1. She was more like a beau - ty queen from a mov - ie scene.
2. For for - ty days and for for - ty nights law was on her side.

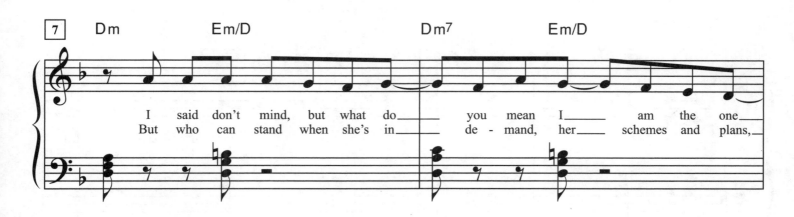

I said don't mind, but what do you mean I am the one
But who can stand when she's in de - mand, her schemes and plans,

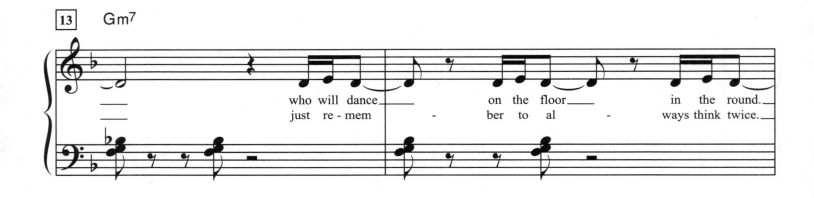

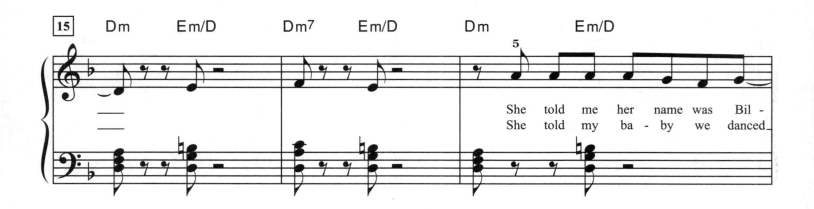

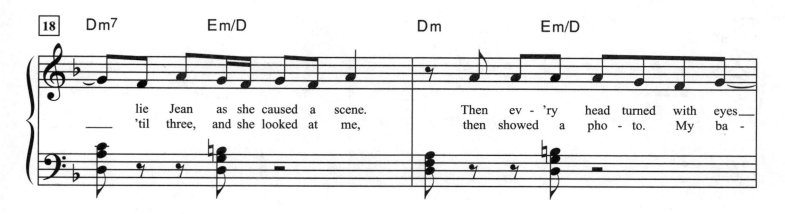

18 Dm7   Em/D   Dm   Em/D

lie Jean as she caused a scene. Then ev - 'ry head turned with eyes___
'til three, and she looked at me, then showed a pho - to. My ba -

20 Dm7   Em/D   Gm7

that dreamed of be - ing the one___ who will dance___
by cried. His eyes were like mine. Can we dance___

22 Dm   Em/D   Dm7   Em/D

on the floor___ in the round.___
on the floor___ in the round?___

Bridge:

25 B♭   Dm

Peo - ple al - ways told me, be care - ful what___ you do, don't

mf

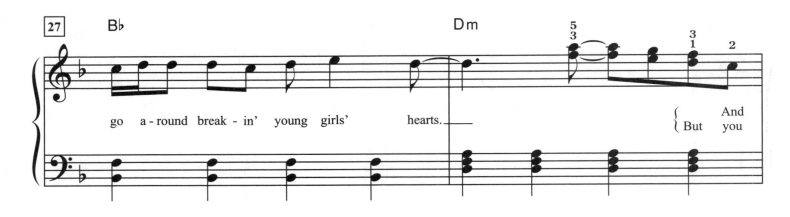

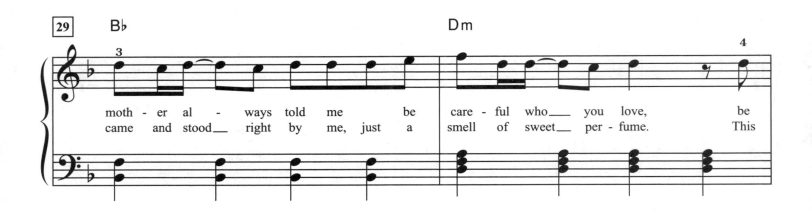

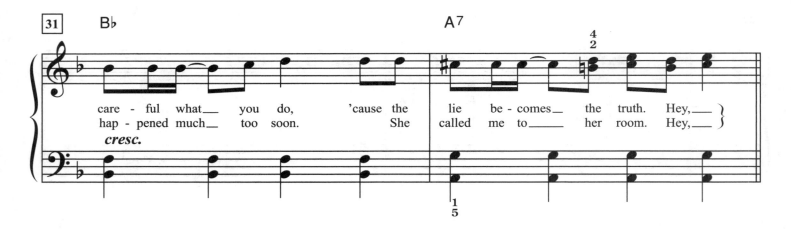

Chorus:

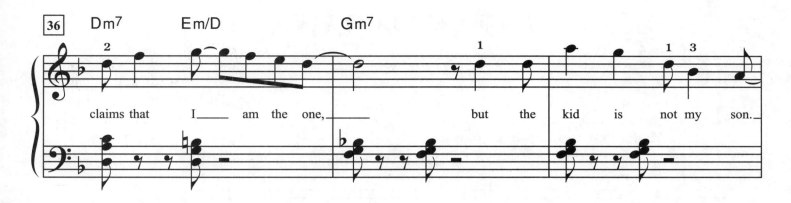

claims that I____ am the one,____ but the kid is not my son.

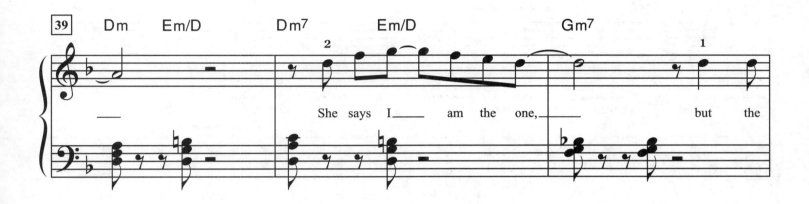

____ She says I____ am the one,____ but the

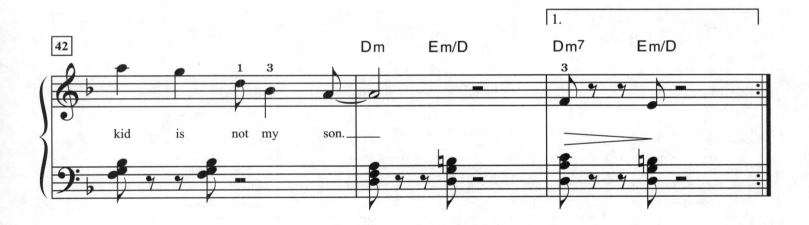

kid is not my son.____

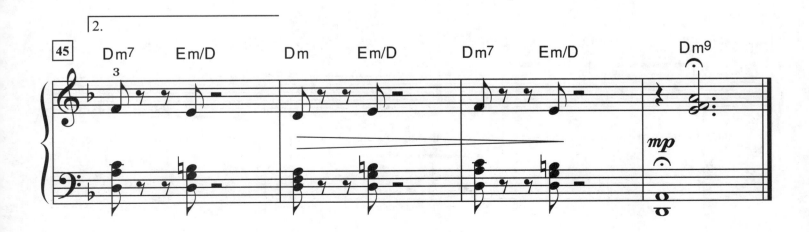

BREAK OF DAWN

Words and Music by
Michael Jackson and Dr. Freeze
Arranged by Dan Coates

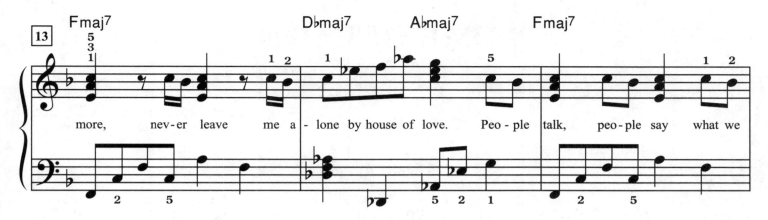
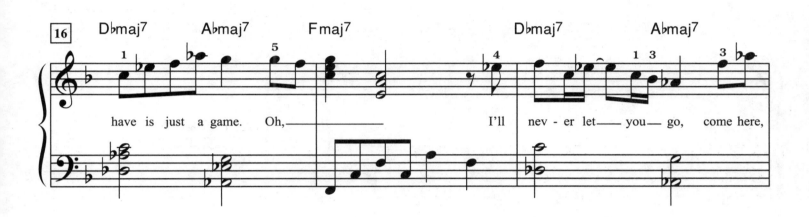
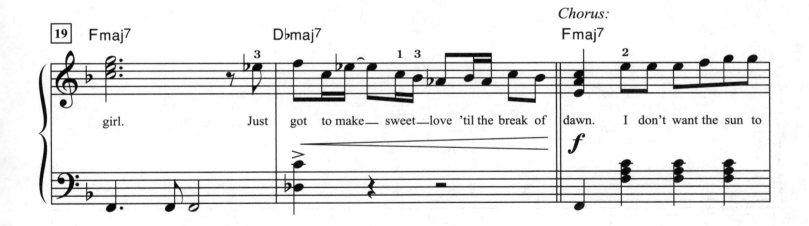
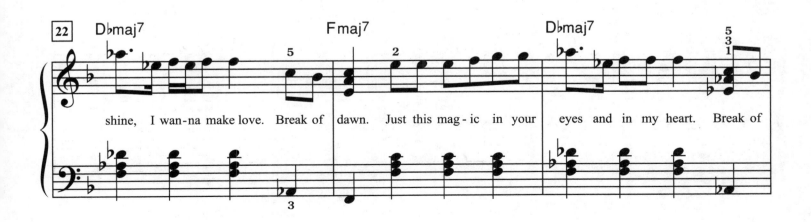

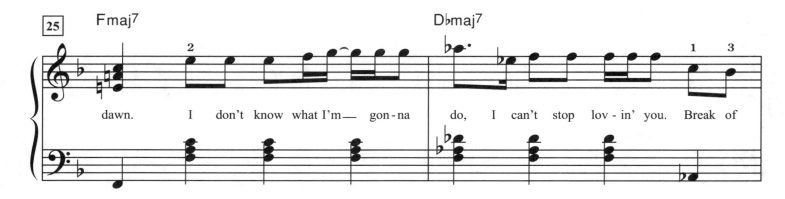

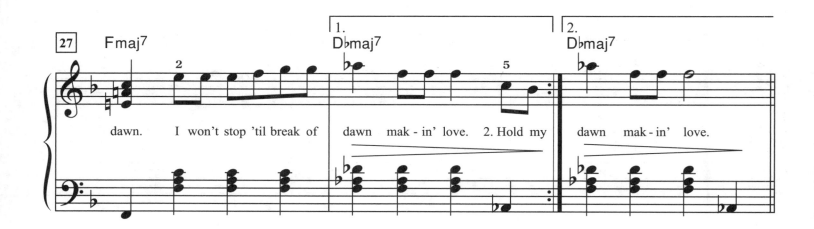

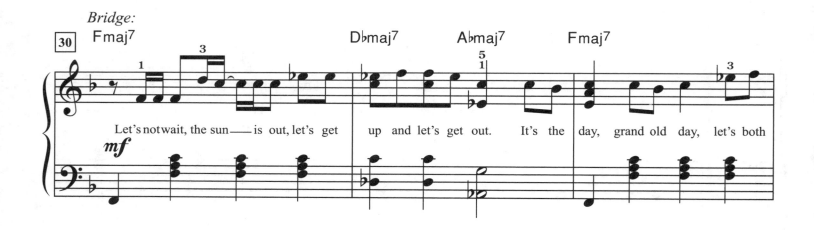

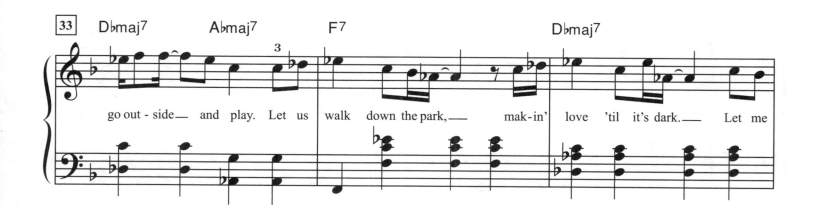

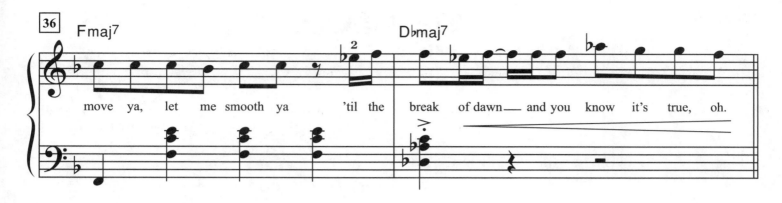

Chorus:

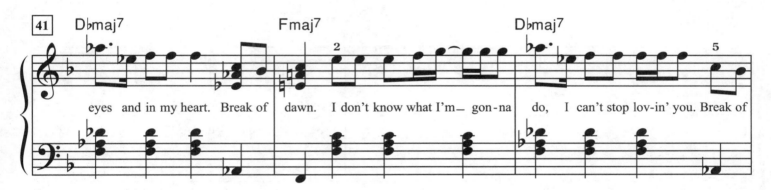

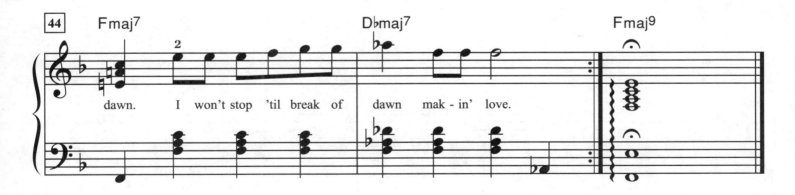

Verse 2:
Hold my hand, feel the sweat,
Yes, you've got me nervous yet.
Let me groove, let me soothe,
Let me take you on a cruise.
There's imagination a-workin',
Never been there before.
Have you ever wanted to dream about those
Things you've never known.
(To Chorus:)

DIRTY DIANA

Written and Composed by Michael Jackson
Arranged by Dan Coates

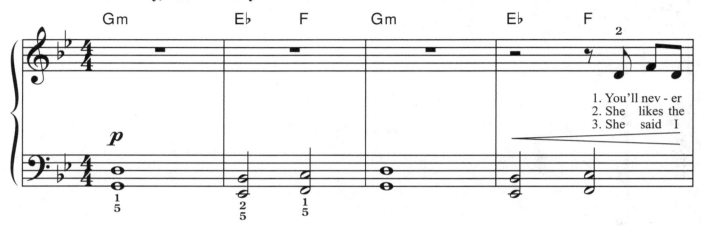

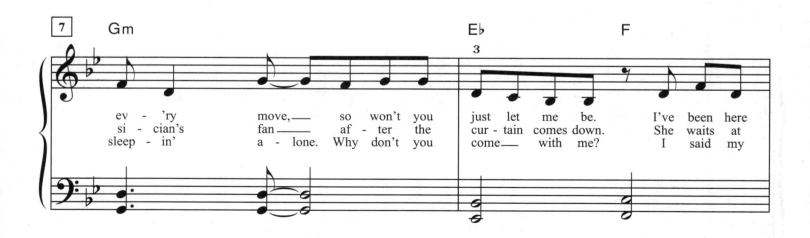

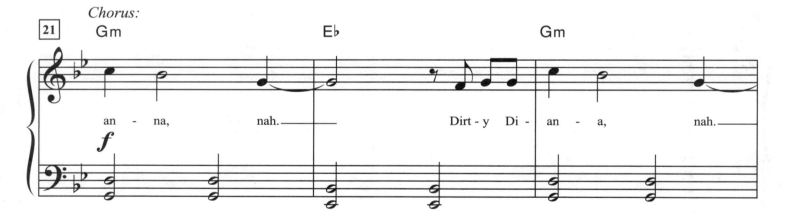

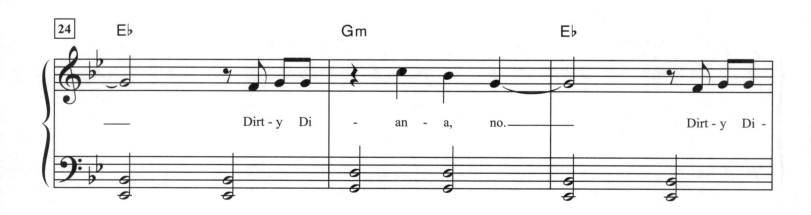

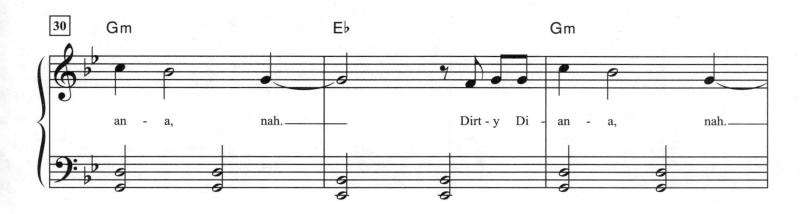

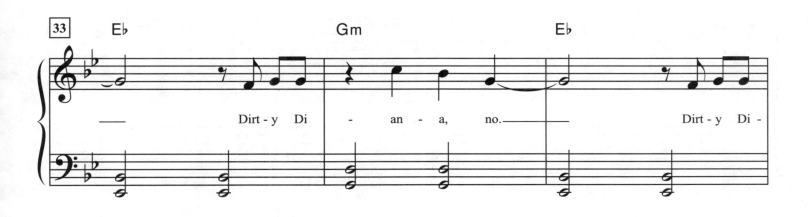

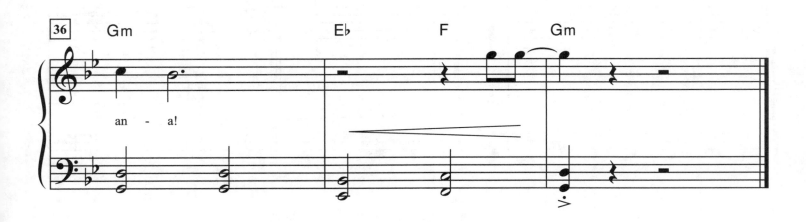

DON'T STOP 'TIL YOU GET ENOUGH

Written and Composed by Michael Jackson
Arranged by Dan Coates

Moderately fast

Verse:

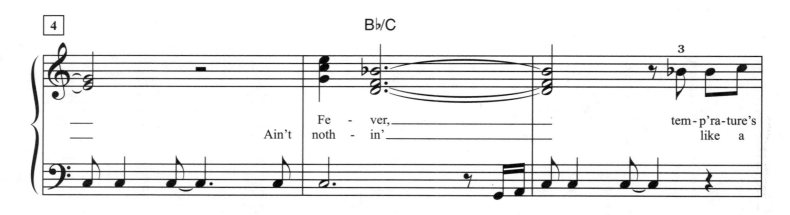

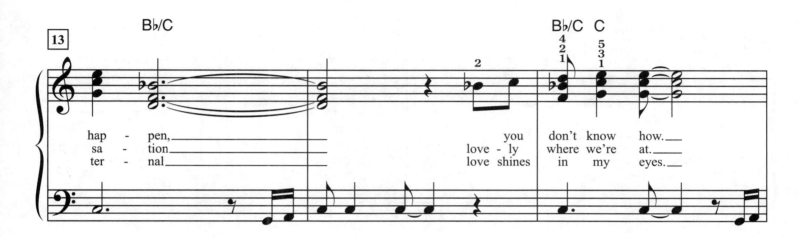

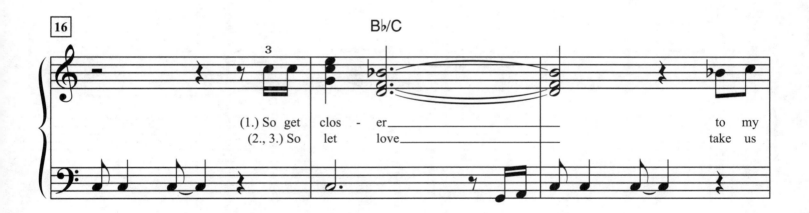

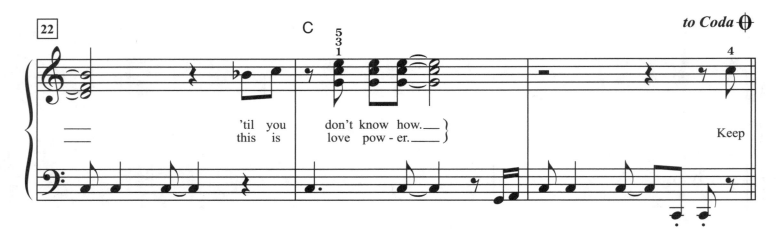

to Coda

Chorus:

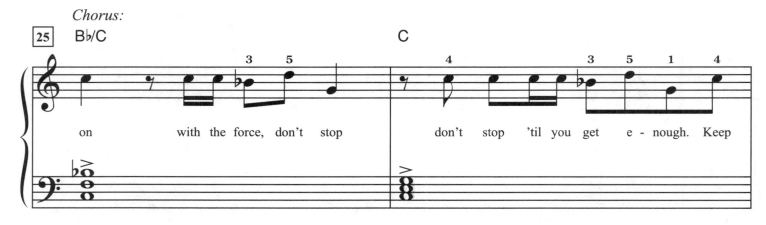

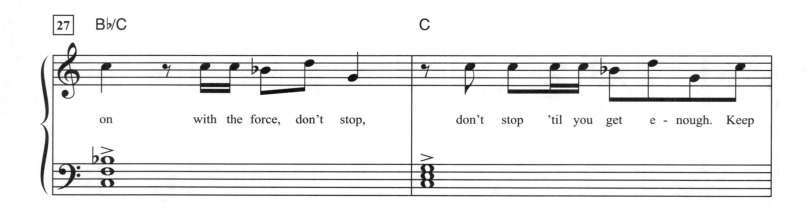

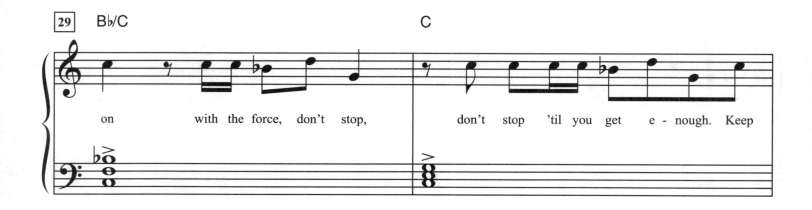

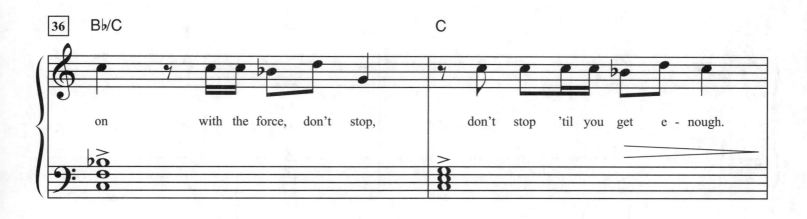

EARTH SONG

Words and Music by Michael Jackson
Arranged by Dan Coates

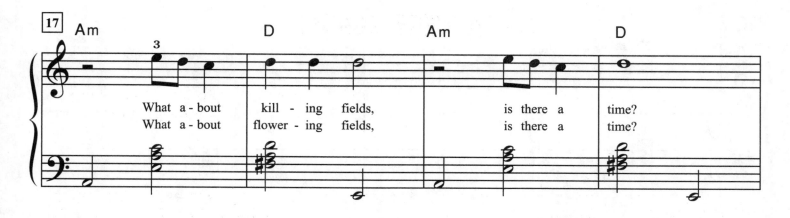

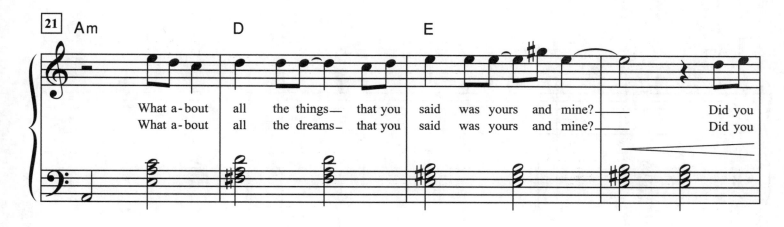

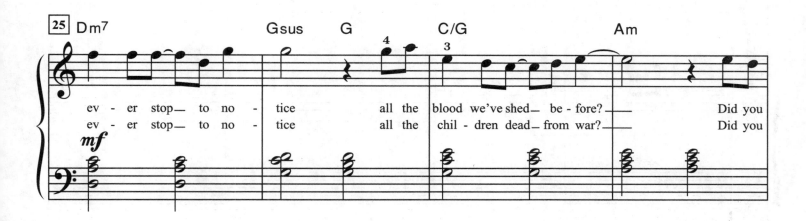

Chorus:

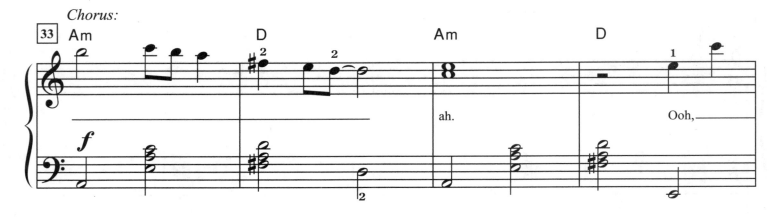

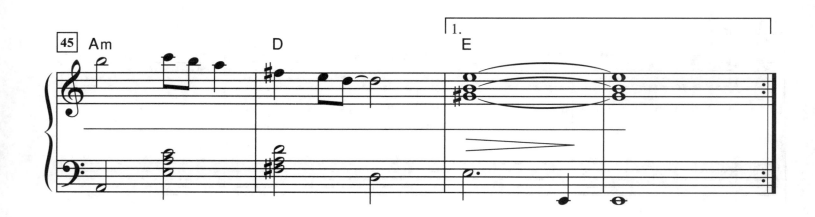

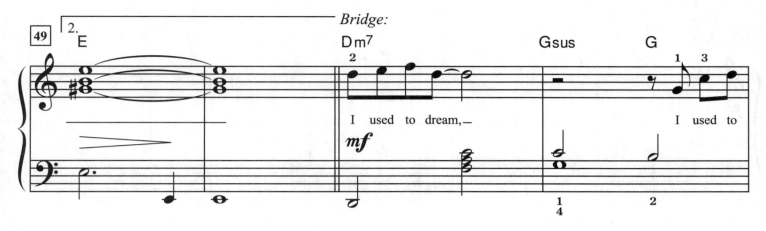

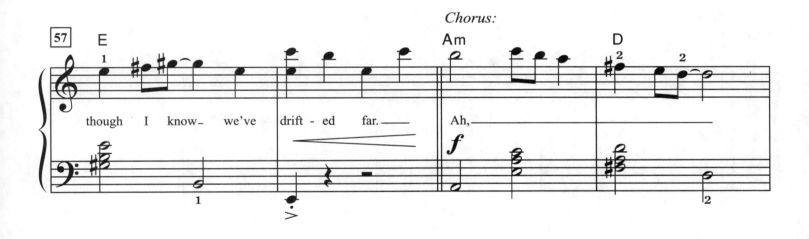

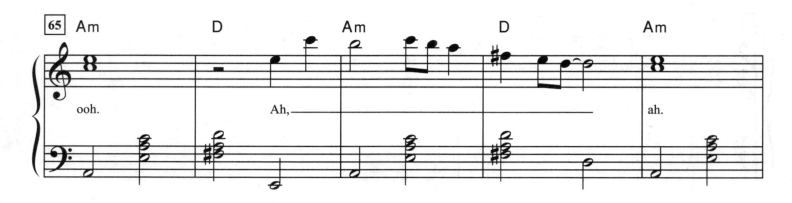

65 | Am — D — Am — D — Am

ooh. Ah,_____ ah.

70 | D — Am — D — E

Ooh._____ Hey._____

Verse:

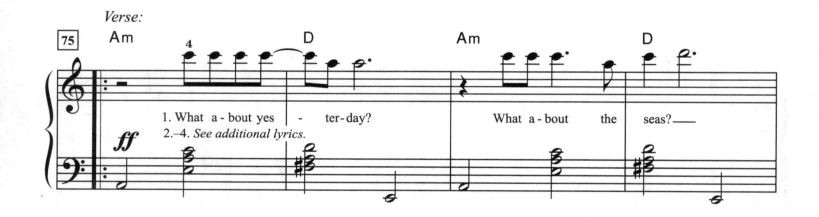

75 | Am — D — Am — D

1. What a-bout yes - ter-day? What a-bout the seas?___
2.–4. *See additional lyrics.*

ff

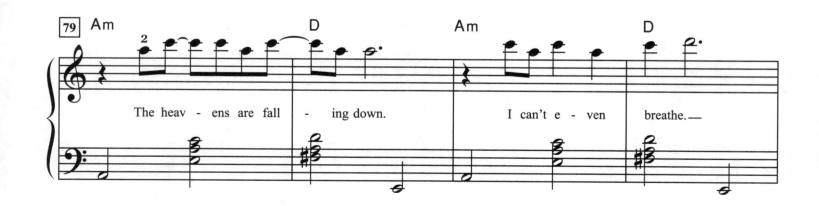

79 | Am — D — Am — D

The heav - ens are fall - ing down. I can't e - ven breathe.___

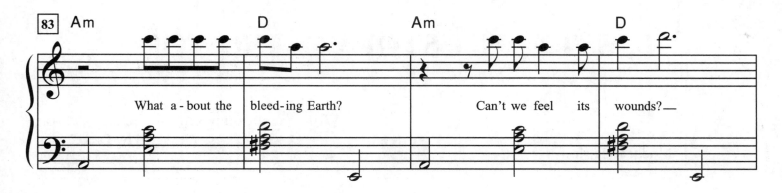

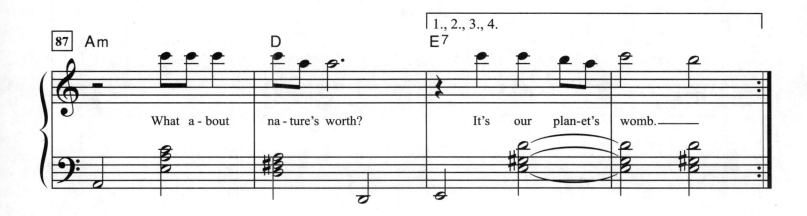

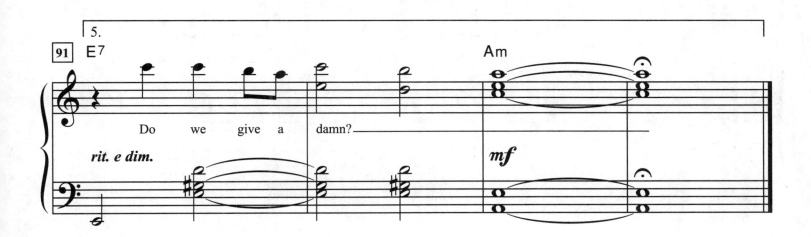

Verse 2:
What about animals?
We've turned kingdom to dust.
What about elephants?
Have we lost their trust?
What about crying whales?
We're ravaging the seas.
What about forest trails,
Burnt despite our pleas?

Verse 3:
What about the holy land
Torn apart by creed?
What about the common man,
Can't we set him free?
What about children cying?
Can't you hear them cry?
Where did we go wrong?
Someone tell me why.

Verse 4:
What about babies?
What about the days?
What about all their joy?
What about the man?
What about the crying man?
What about Abraham?
What about death again?
Do we give a damn?

I JUST CAN'T STOP LOVING YOU

Written and Composed by Michael Jackson
Arranged by Dan Coates

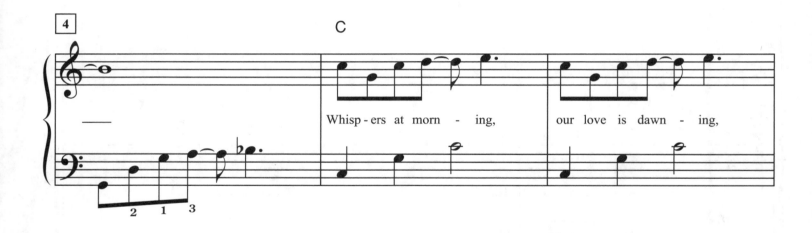

41

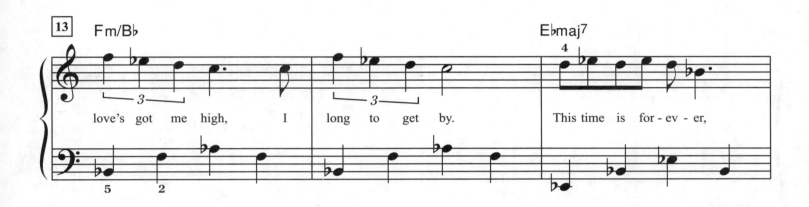

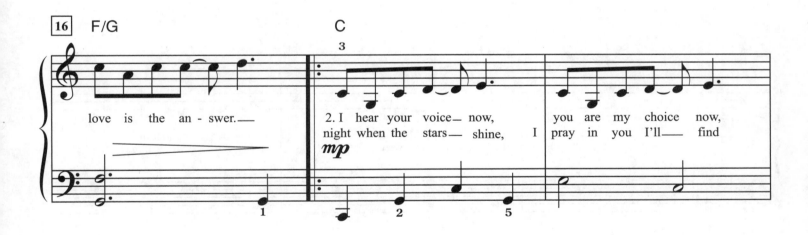

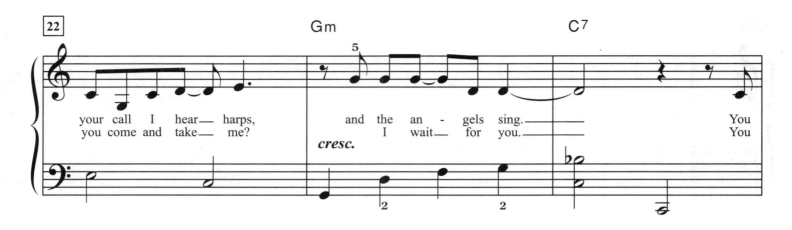

Chorus:

BLACK OR WHITE

Written and Composed by Michael Jackson
Arranged by Dan Coates

think-in' a-bout my ba-by, it don't mat-ter if you're black or white.

1. F/A C/G F6 C/G   2. F/A C/G

F6 C/G F

Now tell me you a-gree with me when I saw you kick-ing dirt in my

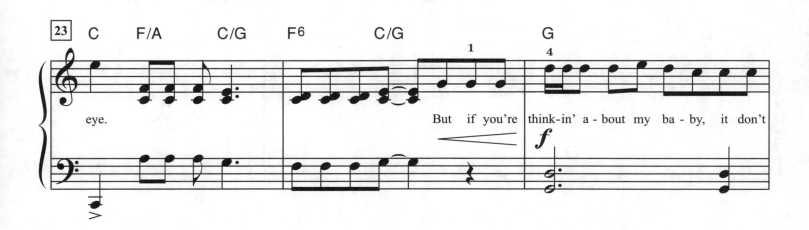

C F/A C/G F6 C/G G

eye.   But if you're think-in' a-bout my ba-by, it don't

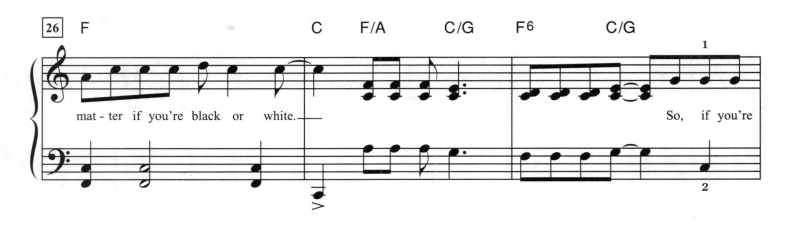

26 F   C   F/A   C/G   F6   C/G

mat - ter if you're black or white.   So, if you're

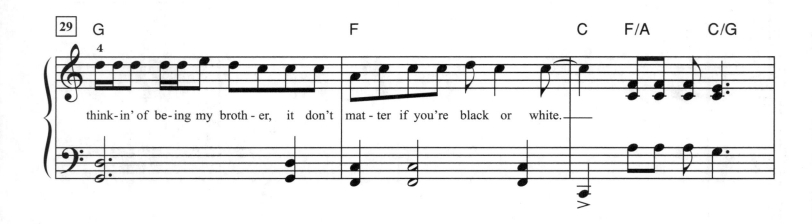

29 G   F   C   F/A   C/G

think-in' of be-ing my broth-er, it don't mat - ter if you're black or white.

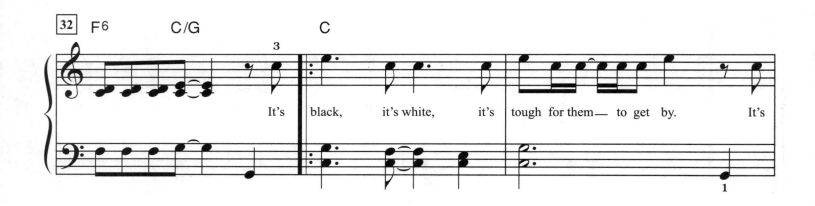

32 F6   C/G   C

It's   black,   it's white,   it's tough for them— to get by.   It's

1. F/C   C   2.   G   C

35

black,   it's white.   It's

MAN IN THE MIRROR

Words and Music by
Siedah Garrett and Glen Ballard
Arranged by Dan Coates

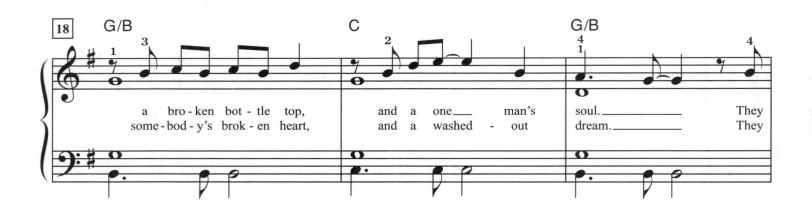

That's why I want you to know: } I'm start-ing with the man in the mir-ror,
That's why I'm start-ing with me.

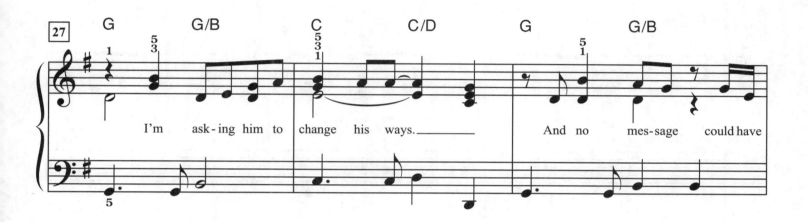

I'm ask-ing him to change his ways._____ And no mes-sage could have

been an - y clear - er: If you wan - na make the world a bet - ter place, take a

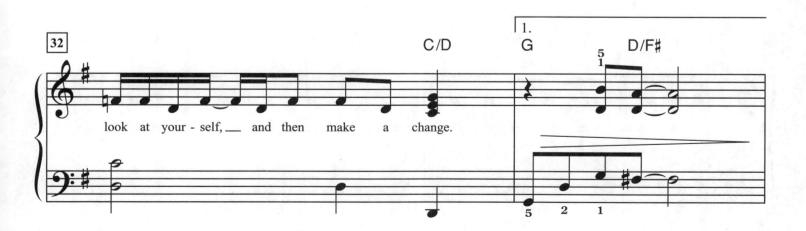

look at your - self,__ and then make a change.

Na na na, na na na, na na na na.

I'm start-ing with the man in the mir-ror, I'm ask-ing him to

change his ways. And no mes-sage could have been an-y clear-er: If you

wan-na make the world a bet-ter place, take a look at your-self and then make the change. You got-ta

get it right___ while you got the time,___ 'cause when you close your heart___ then you close your

mind!

Na na na, na na na,___ na na___ na na.___

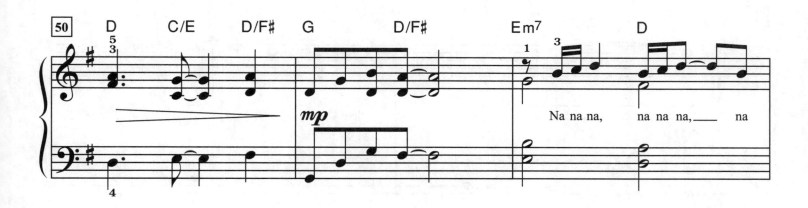

Na na na, na na na,___ na

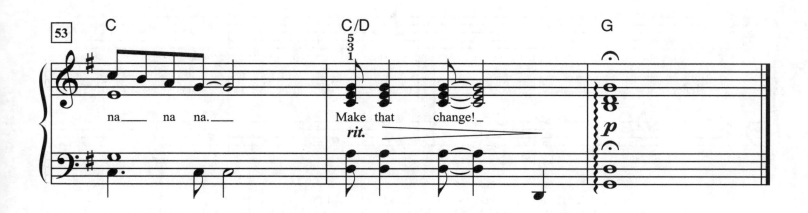

na___ na na.___ Make that change!___

ONE MORE CHANCE

Words and Music by R. Kelly
Arranged by Dan Coates

53

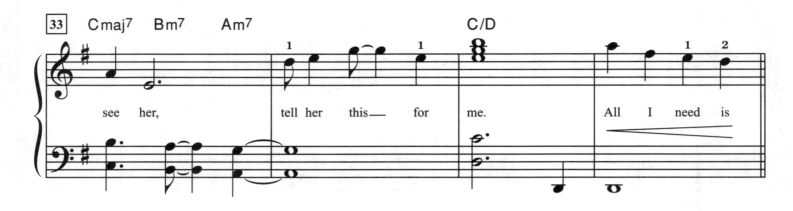

see her, tell her this— for me. All I need is

Chorus:

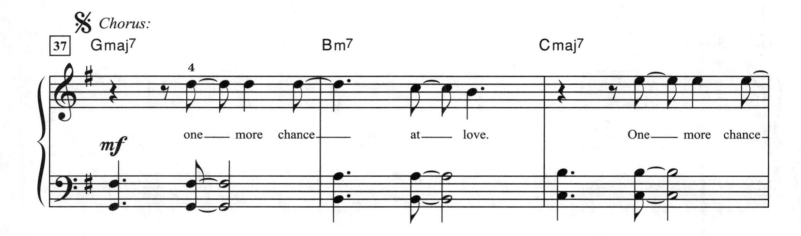

one— more chance— at— love. One— more chance—

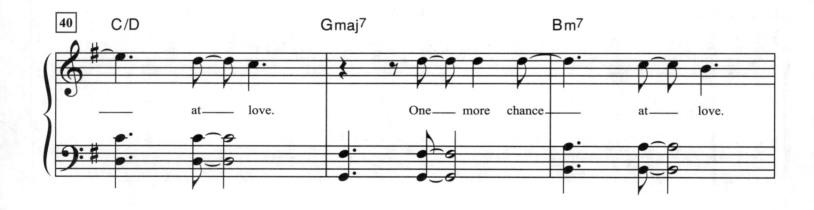

— at— love. One— more chance— at— love.

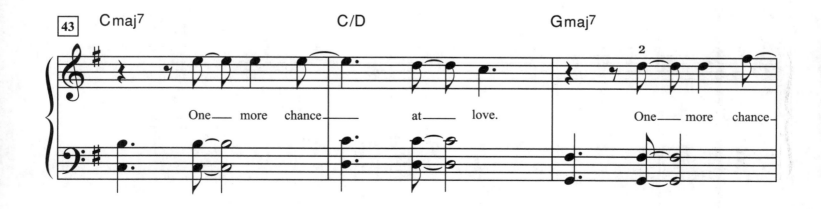

One— more chance— at— love. One— more chance—

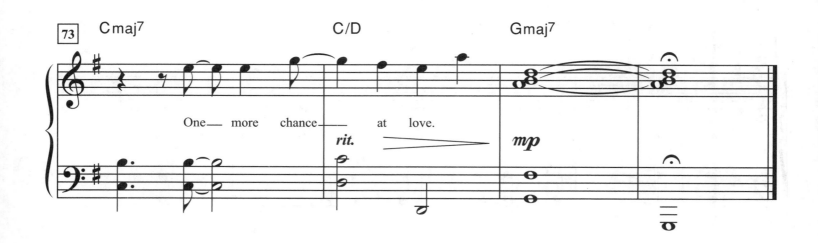

ROCK WITH YOU

Words and Music by Rod Temperton
Arranged by Dan Coates

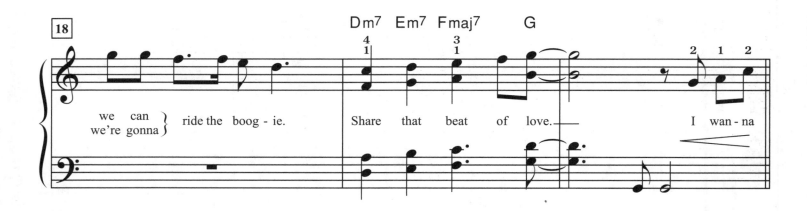

℅ *Chorus:*

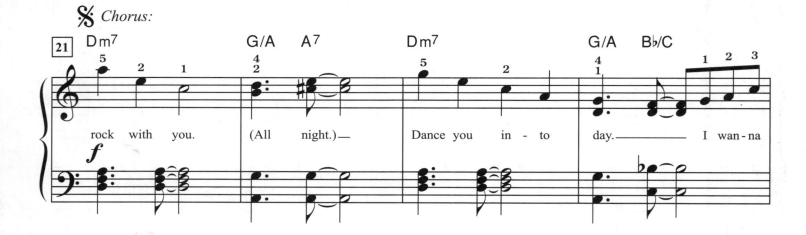

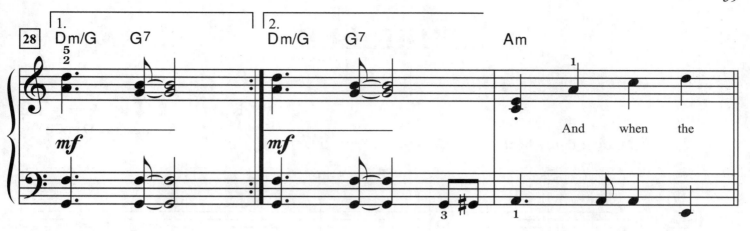

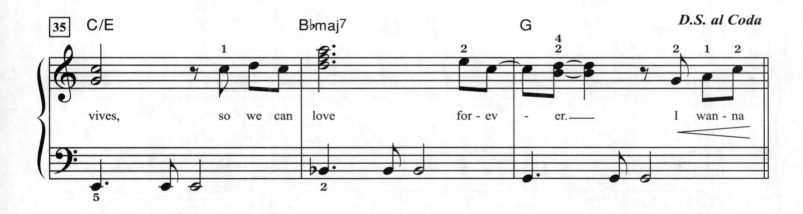

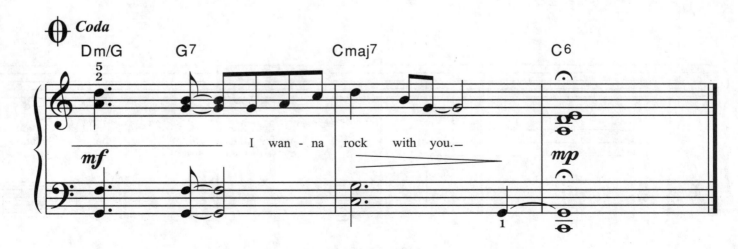

THRILLER

Words and Music by Rod Temperton
Arranged by Dan Coates

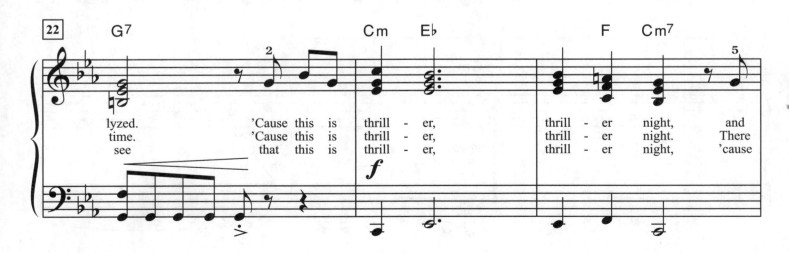

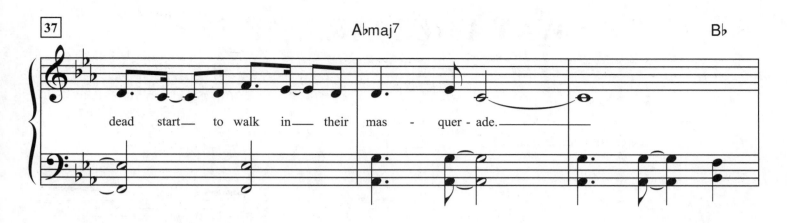

dead start— to walk in— their mas - quer - ade.—

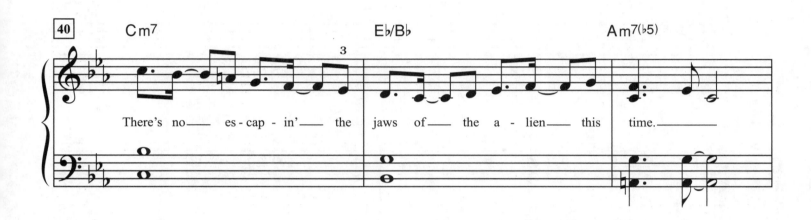

There's no— es - cap - in'— the jaws of — the a - lien— this time.—

D.S. al Coda

This is the end of your life.

Coda

night.

ff

THE WAY YOU MAKE ME FEEL

Written and Composed by Michael Jackson
Arranged by Dan Coates

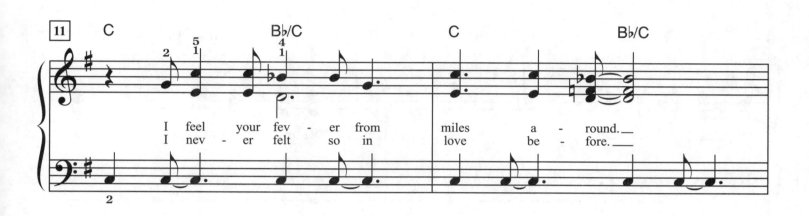

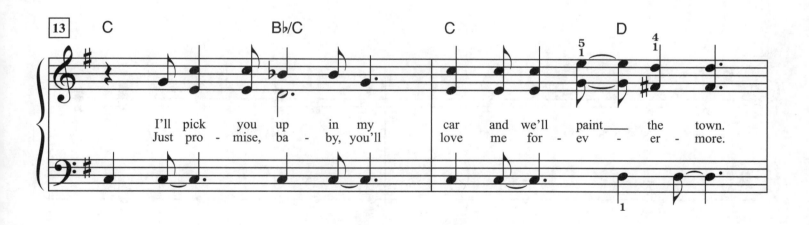

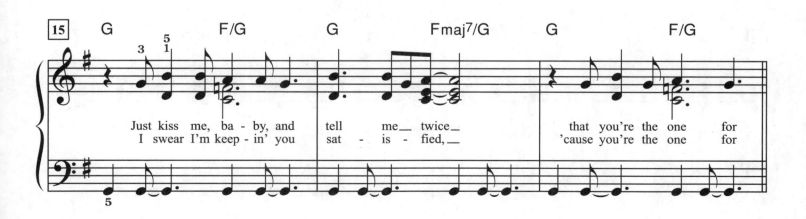

Chorus:

The way you make me feel, *(The way you make me feel,*

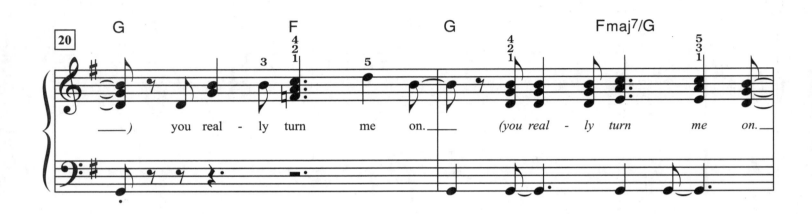

___) you real - ly turn me on. *(you real - ly turn me on.*

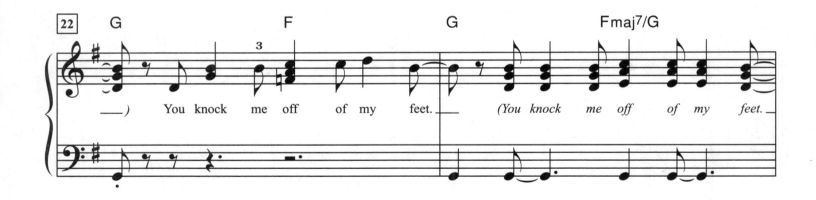

___) You knock me off of my feet. *(You knock me off of my feet.*

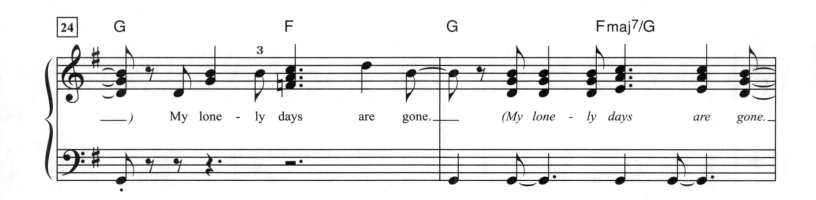

___) My lone - ly days are gone. *(My lone - ly days are gone.*

YOU ARE NOT ALONE

Words and Music by R. Kelly
Arranged by Dan Coates

Chorus:

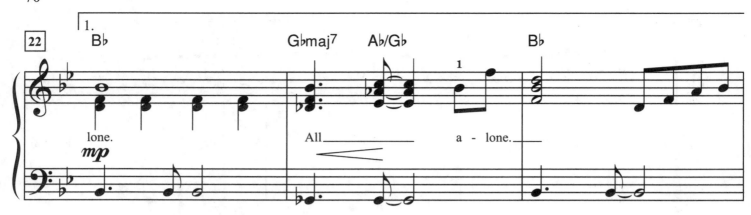

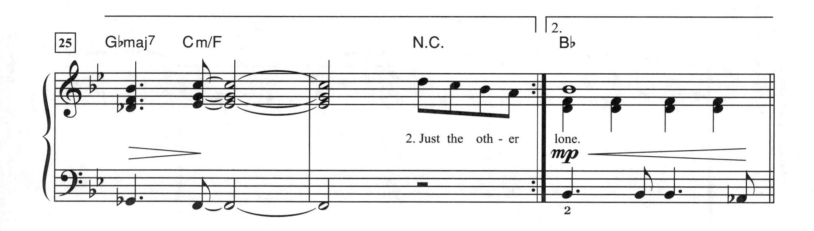

Bridge:

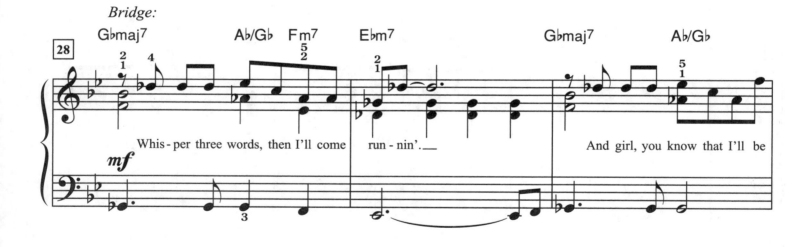

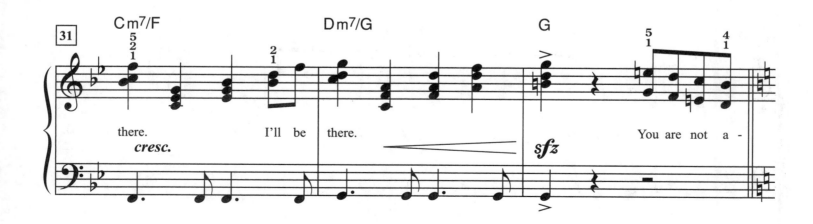

Chorus:

lone,   I am here with you.   Though you're far a - way,   I am here to

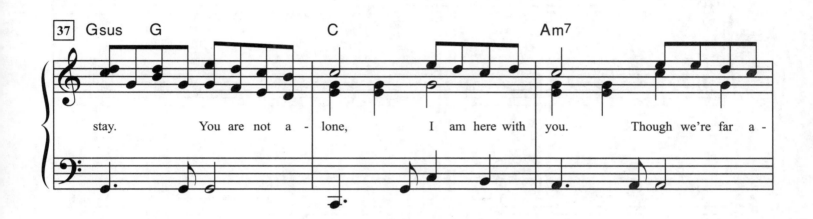

stay.   You are not a - lone,   I am here with you.   Though we're far a -

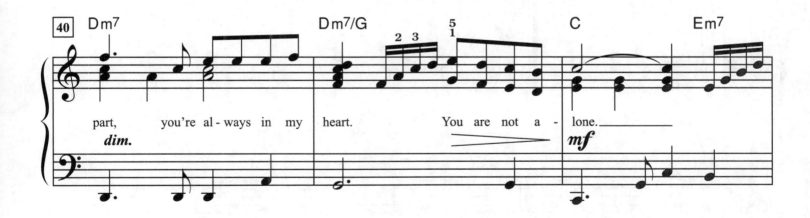

part,   you're al - ways in my heart.   You are not a - lone.

You are not a - lone.

YOU ROCK MY WORLD

Words and Music by Michael Jackson, Rodney Jerkins,
Fred Jerkins III, Lashawn Daniels and Nora Payne
Arranged by Dan Coates

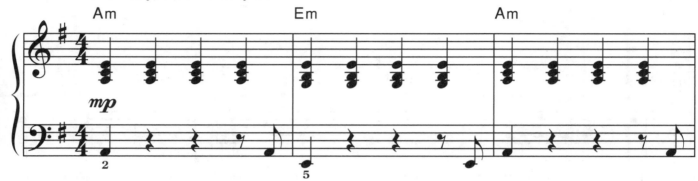

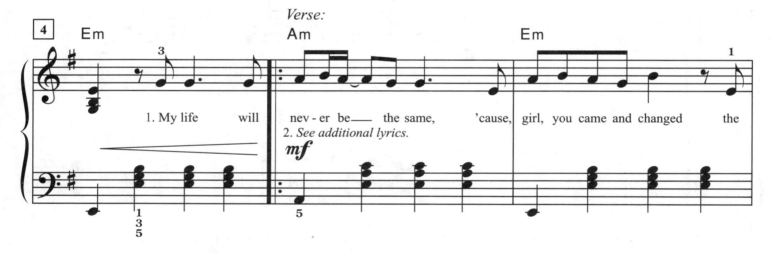

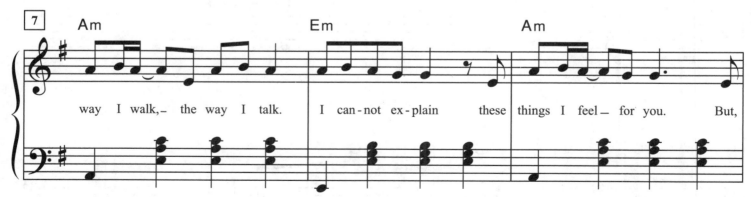

Verse 2:
In time, I knew that love would bring
Such happiness to me.
I tried to keep my sanity.
I've waited patiently.
Girl, you know it seems
My life is so complete.
A love that's true because of you.
Keep doing what you do.
Think that I found the perfct love
I've searched for all my life.
(Searched for all my life.)
Think I'd find such a perfect love
That's awesomely so right, girl.
(To Chorus:)

SMOOTH CRIMINAL

Written and Composed by Michael Jackson
Arranged by Dan Coates

Moderately, with a steady beat

1. As he came in-to the win-dow it was the sound of a cre-scen-do.

He came in-to her a-part-ment, he left the blood-stains on the car-pet.

She ran un-der-neath the ta-ble, he could see she was un-a-ble.
2. So they came in-to the out-way, it was Sun-day. What a black day.

So she ran in-to the bed-room, she was struck down. It was her doom.
Mouth to mouth re-sus-ci-ta-tion, sound-ing heart-beats in-tim-i-da-tions.

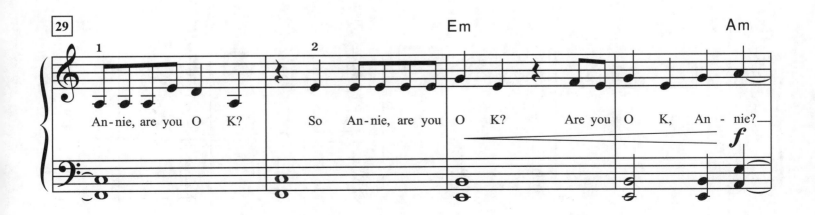

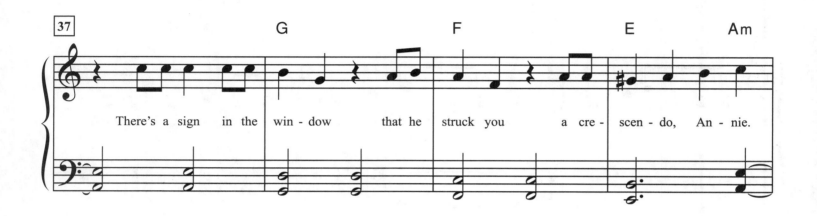

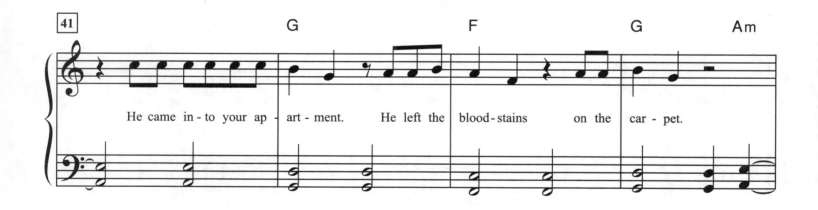

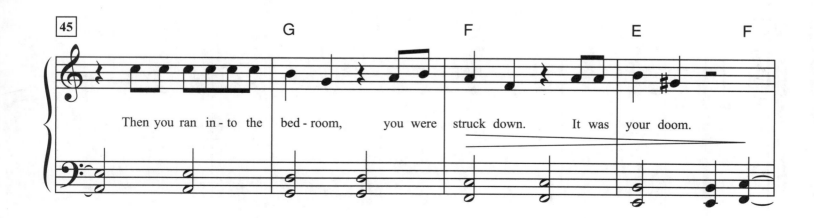